Written by
Nicola
Chave

Like Yours, Like Mine

SKIN

KidHaven
PUBLISHING

Published in 2027 by
KidHaven Publishing, an Imprint of Greenhaven Publishing, LLC
2544 Clinton St., Buffalo, NY 14224

Written by: Nicola Chave
Edited by: Beth Latham
Designed by: Ian McMullen

All facts, statistics, web addresses, and URLs in this book were verified as valid and accurate at time of writing. No responsibility for any changes to external websites or references can be accepted by either the author or publisher.

Cataloging-in-Publication Data

Names: Chave, Nicola.
Title: Skin / Nicola Chave.
Description: Buffalo, NY : KidHaven Publishing, 2027. | Series: Like yours, like mine | Includes glossary and index.
Identifiers: ISBN 9781534570948 (pbk.) | ISBN 9781534570955 (library bound) | ISBN 9781534570962 (ebook)
Subjects: LCSH: Skin--Juvenile literature.
Classification: LCC QP88.5 C438 2027 | DDC 612.79--dc23

Printed in the United States

CPSIA compliance information: Batch #CS27KH: For further information contact Greenhaven Publishing LLC at 1-844-317-7404.

Please visit our website,
www.greenhavenpublishing.com.
For a free color catalog of all our high-quality books,
call toll free 1-844-317-7404
or fax 1-844-317-7405.

Find us on

Image Credits
Images courtesy of Shutterstock.com, unless otherwise stated.
Cover - Air Images, Julaix, Chay_Tee.
4-5 - Chay_Tee, Gelpi. 6-7 - wavebreakmedia, PeopleImages. 8-9 - Xavier Lorenzo, Natasha Zakharova. 10-11 - Pixel-Shot, Chechotkin, Dr. Ye. 12-13 - Sharomka, wsetiawan, Demkat, phBodrova, jaojormami. 14-15 - AmpYang Images, TY Lim, ChrisGreenTea, Arthito. 16-17 - Roman Samborskyi, GENERAL STOCKIN, Funtasy Developer, Seamm. 18-19 - NeonShot, Bricolage, Roylan Tkg, DenisProduction.com. 20-21 - ChameleonsEye, Dan Gutu, Pixel-Shot. 22-23 - PeopleImages, pics five.

CONTENTS

Words that look like **THIS** can be found in the glossary on page 24.

AMAZING SKIN

Our world is amazing, and so are we! Billions of people live on our planet, and every single person is **UNIQUE**. No two people are exactly alike. That is what makes us so special.

Let's explore the wonderful world of human skin!

Our skin is part of what makes us who we are. It covers us from our head to our toes and helps to protect our bodies. Every person's skin is a different color and **TEXTURE**.

COLOR

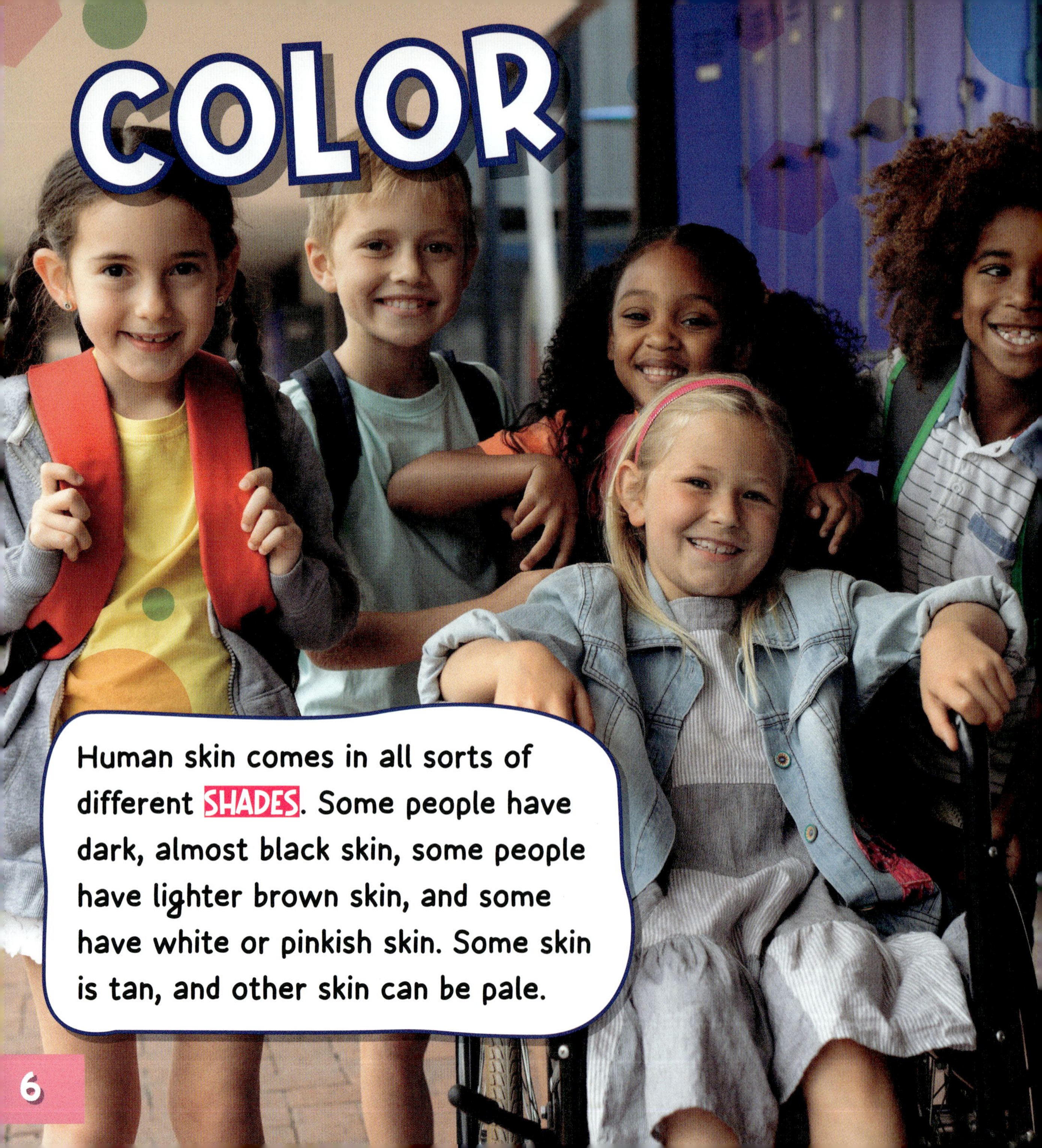

Human skin comes in all sorts of different **SHADES**. Some people have dark, almost black skin, some people have lighter brown skin, and some have white or pinkish skin. Some skin is tan, and other skin can be pale.

You might have similar skin to your friends and family, or it might be very different. Even skin that looks the same as somebody else's is actually unique. Undertones and sun exposure can make the same skin color look different.

AN UNDERTONE IS THE **NATURAL** SHADE OF YOUR SKIN BELOW THE SURFACE.

VITILIGO

Sometimes, a person's skin might be made up of patches of different colors. This is called vitiligo. Vitiligo is a skin **CONDITION** where areas of skin lose their color over time and turn white or pink.

Vitiligo is not dangerous or **CONTAGIOUS**.

OILY OR DRY?

Does your skin feel oily or dry? Oily skin might look shiny and feel greasy. Dry skin might be flaky and peel or look ashy. Dry skin usually needs more moisturizing to keep it healthy.

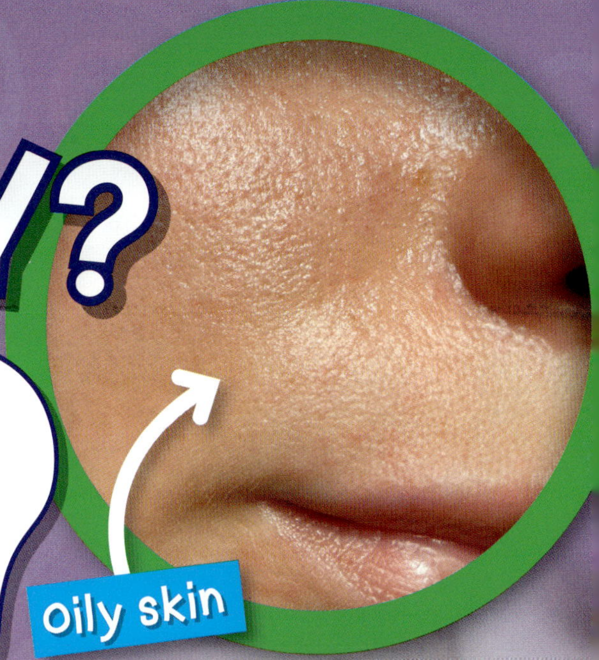

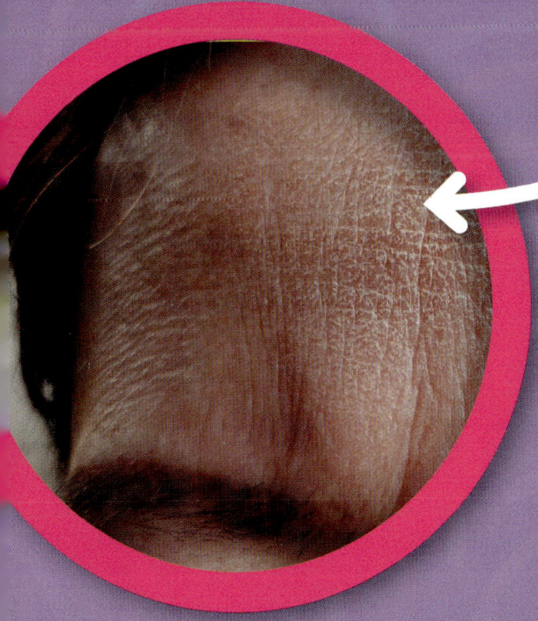

Moisturizer is a cream that people put on their skin to help with dryness.

PIMPLES

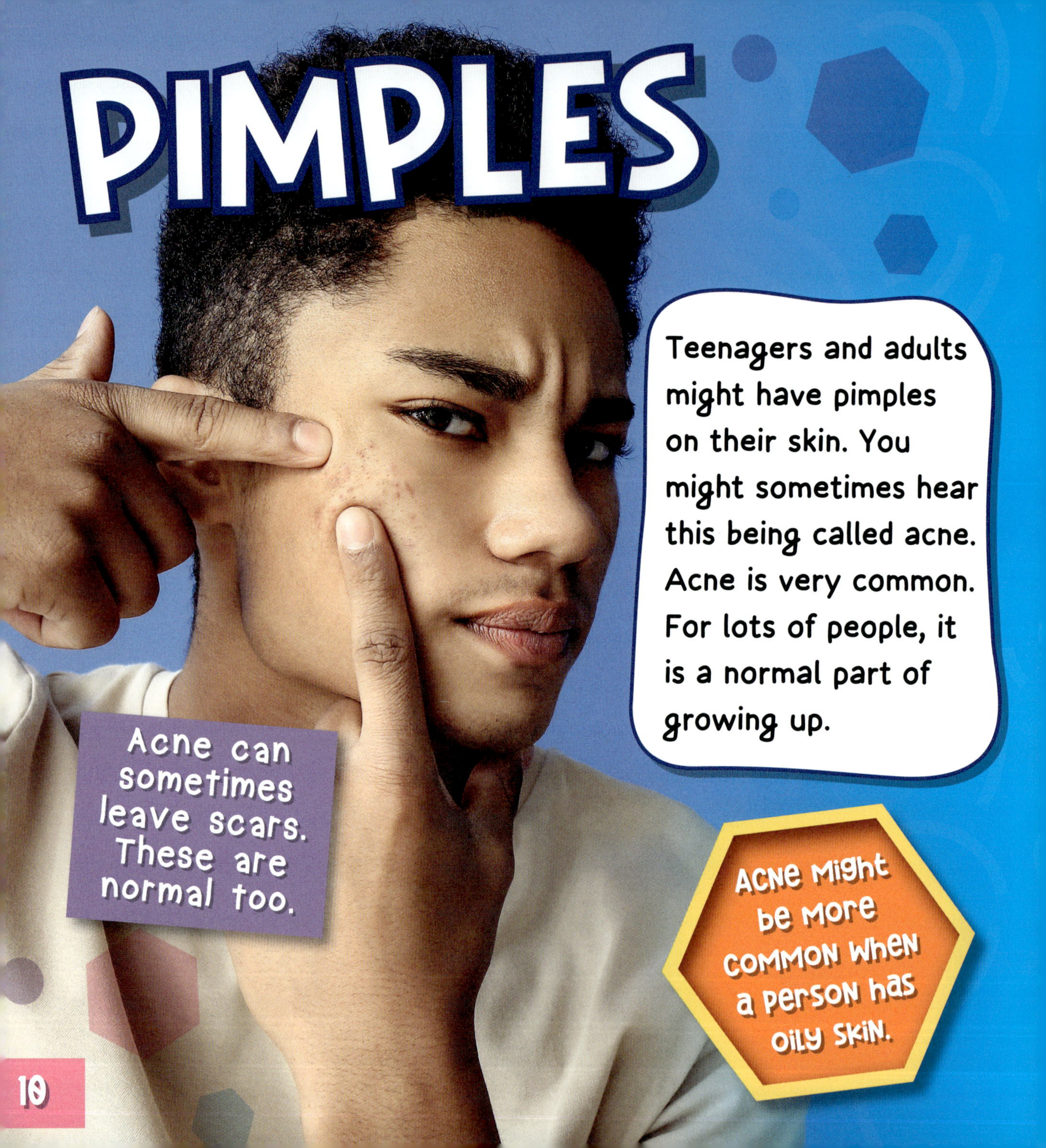

Teenagers and adults might have pimples on their skin. You might sometimes hear this being called acne. Acne is very common. For lots of people, it is a normal part of growing up.

Acne can sometimes leave scars. These are normal too.

Acne might be more common when a person has oily skin.

Pimples usually appear on a person's face, but they can also be on a person's back, chest, and other parts of their body. Sometimes pimples go away on their own, but sometimes they don't.

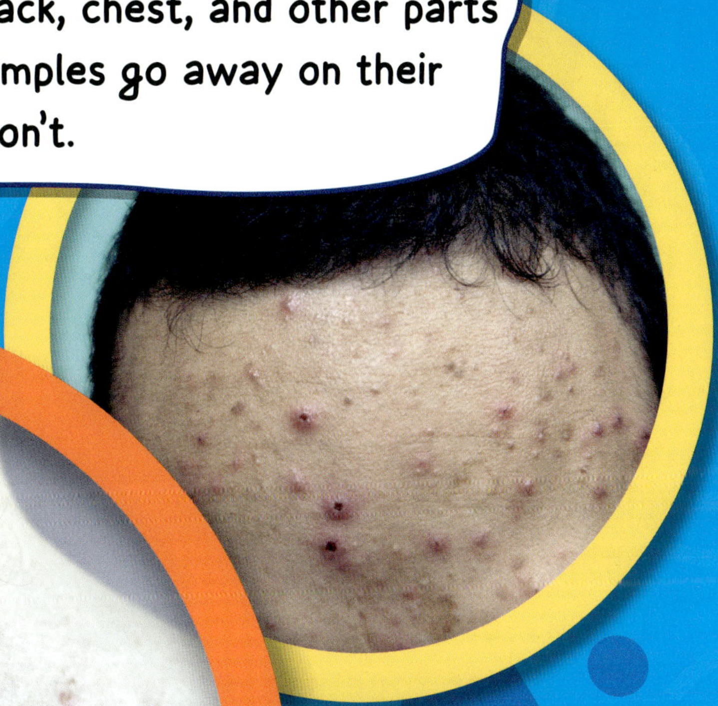

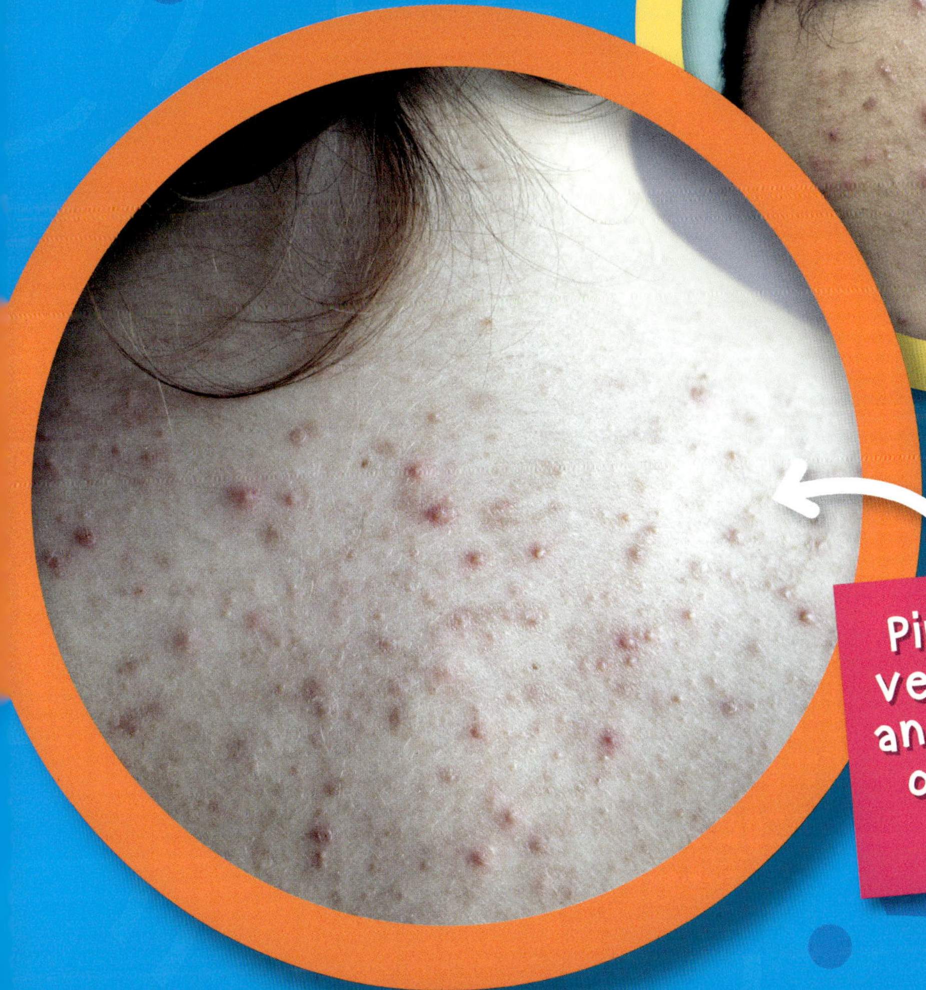

Pimples are very normal, and they are often part of life.

FRECKLES, MOLES, AND BIRTHMARKS

Some people have freckles, moles, or birthmarks on their skin. Freckles are small, brown spots. There are usually lots of them close together. Moles are bigger and more spread out on the body.

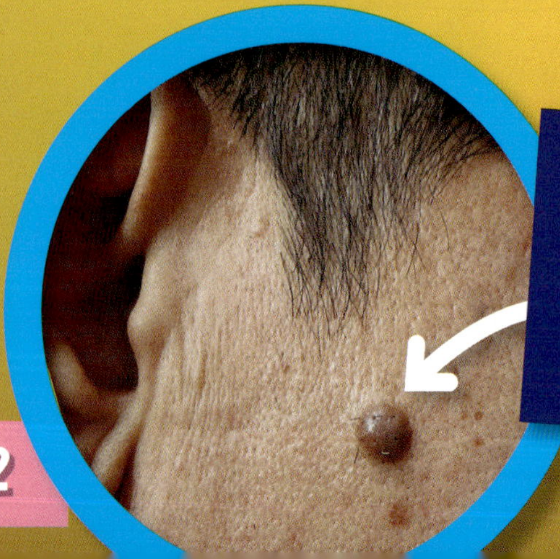

Moles can be small and flat or large and raised.

Birthmarks can come in lots of different colors. They can appear anywhere on a person's skin. Port wine stains are flat red or purple marks. Café-au-lait spots are the color of milky coffee.

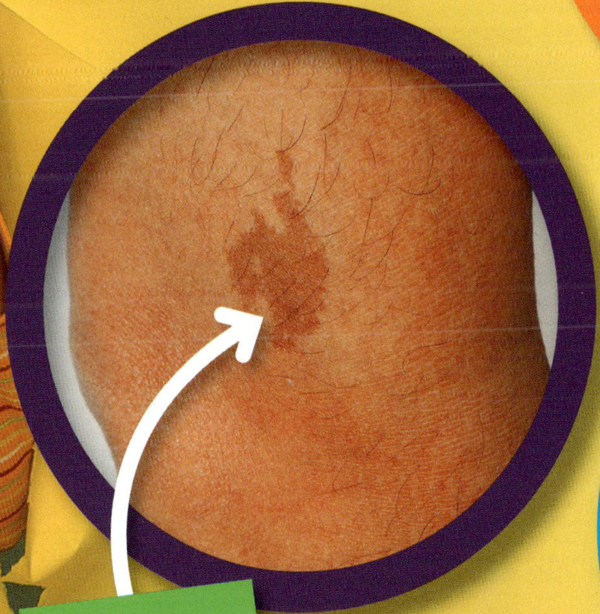

SKIN CONDITIONS

Many people deal with skin conditions during their lives. Lots of children have a skin condition called eczema. Eczema is a type of rash that makes the skin dry, itchy, and red.

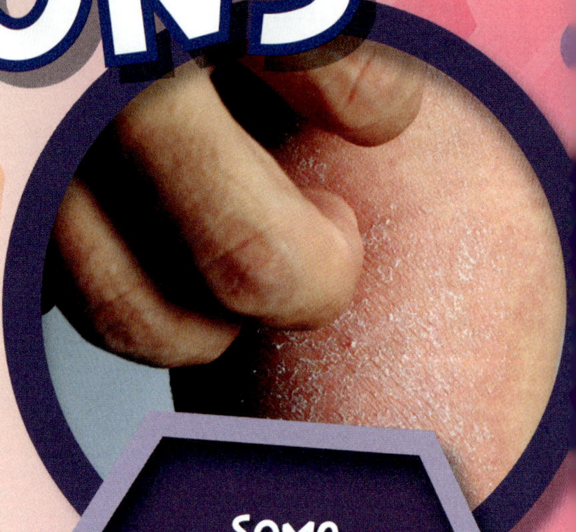

Some rashes can be caused by illnesses and **ALLERGIC REACTIONS**.

Special creams can make eczema less red and itchy.

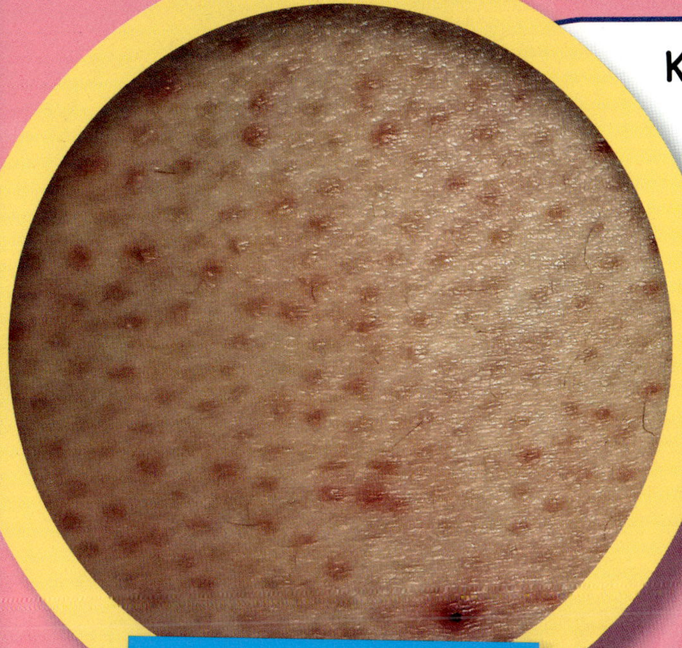

Keratosis pilaris is another skin condition. People with keratosis pilaris have small bumps that appear on their skin.

Keratosis pilaris

Dandruff

Dandruff causes white or gray flakes of skin to appear on someone's head. Special shampoo can make dandruff better.

SCARS

Sometimes, after a cut or a burn on someone's skin **HEALS**, it might turn into a scar. Scars are often raised. They might be white, pink, black, or brown.

Scars stay forever, but sometimes they might fade and become more difficult to notice. Scars show us how amazing our bodies are and how good our skin is at fixing itself.

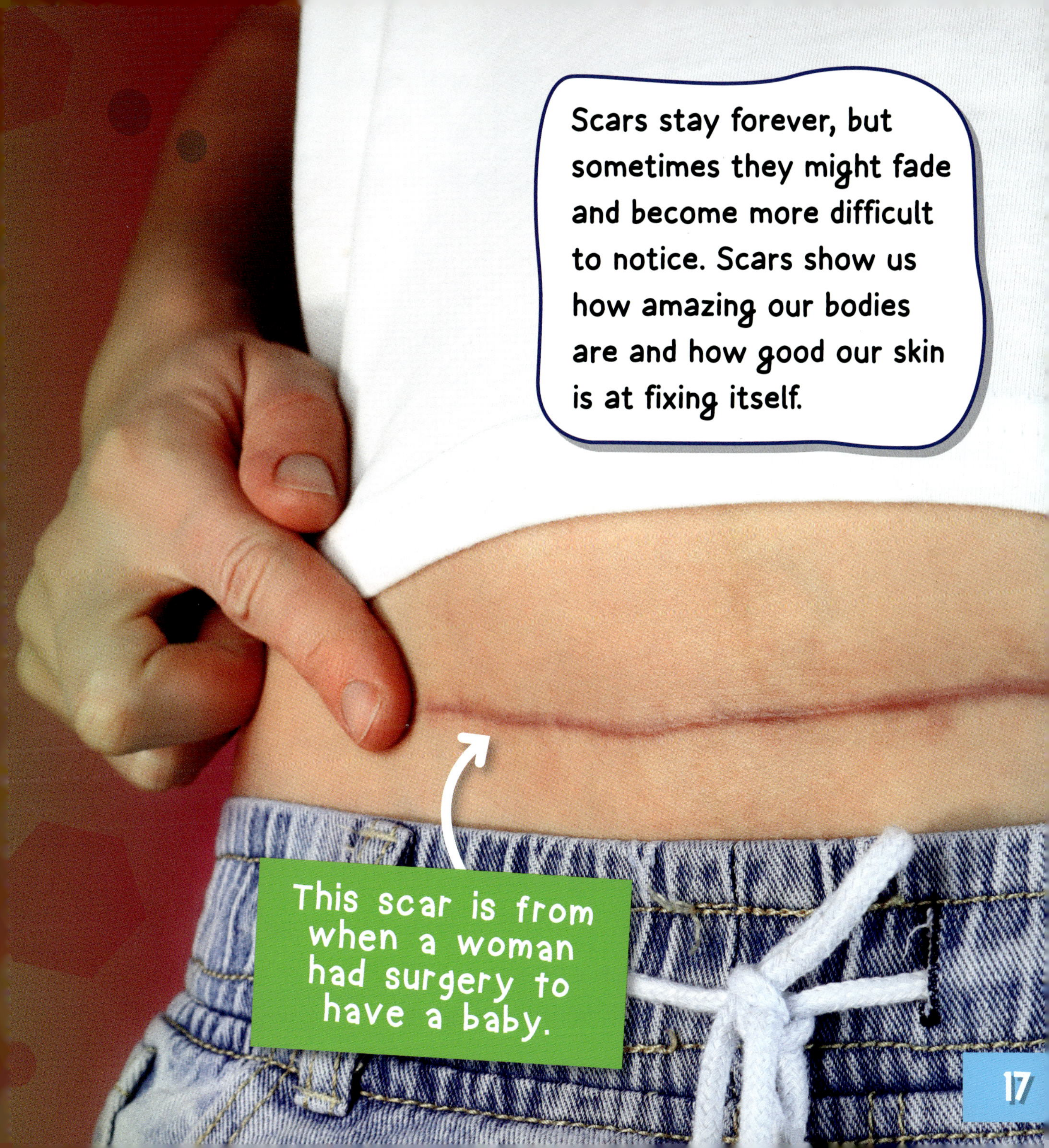

WRINKLES

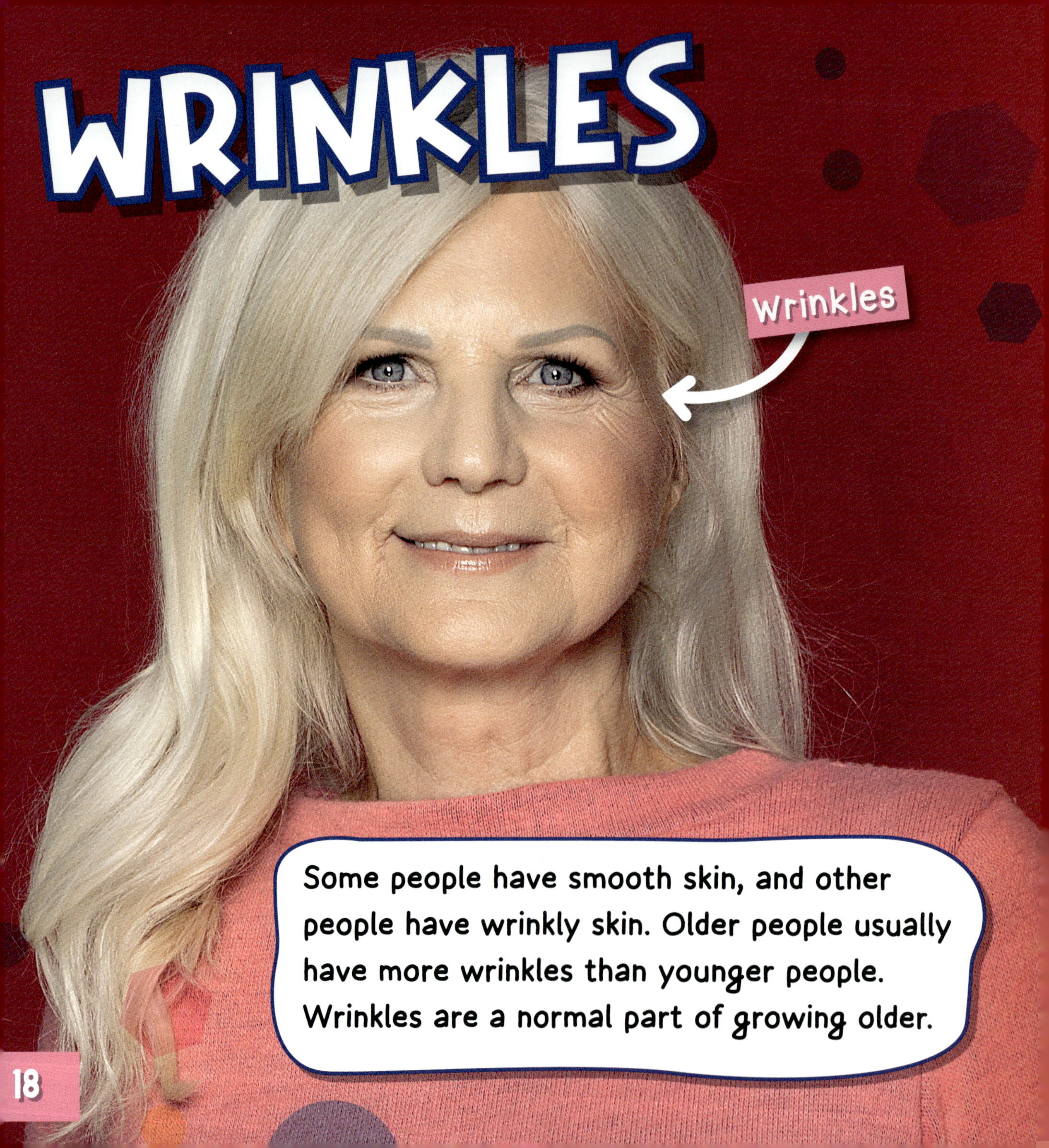

Some people have smooth skin, and other people have wrinkly skin. Older people usually have more wrinkles than younger people. Wrinkles are a normal part of growing older.

As you get older, your skin becomes drier, thinner, and less stretchy. Wrinkles and lines show the lives we have lived and the fun we have had. Some wrinkles are even called laugh lines!

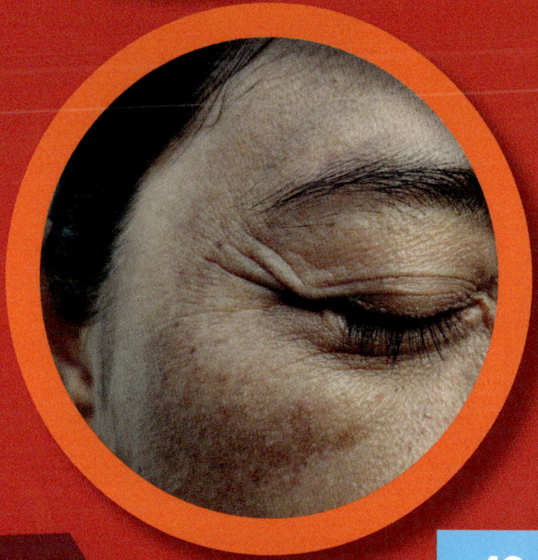

TATTOOS

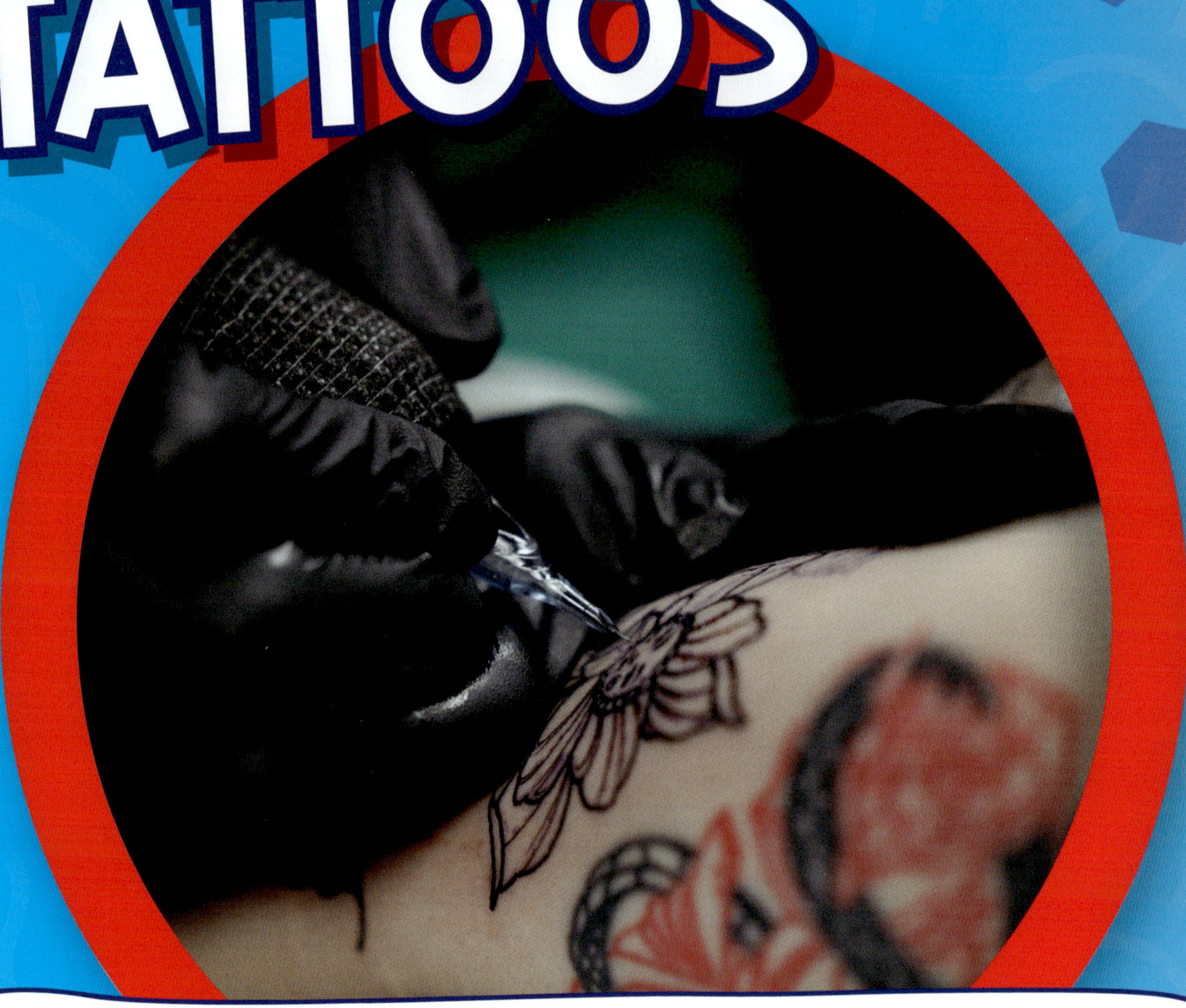

Some adults decorate their skin to express themselves. Tattoos are words or pictures that are added to skin. Adults might use tattoos to show off their **PERSONALITY** or their **CULTURE**.

It is very important that tattoos are done safely. Tattoo artists make sure that they do not damage the person's skin. Fresh tattoos need to be taken care of, or they might become **INFECTED.**

Tā moko tattooing is important to the Māori people of New Zealand.

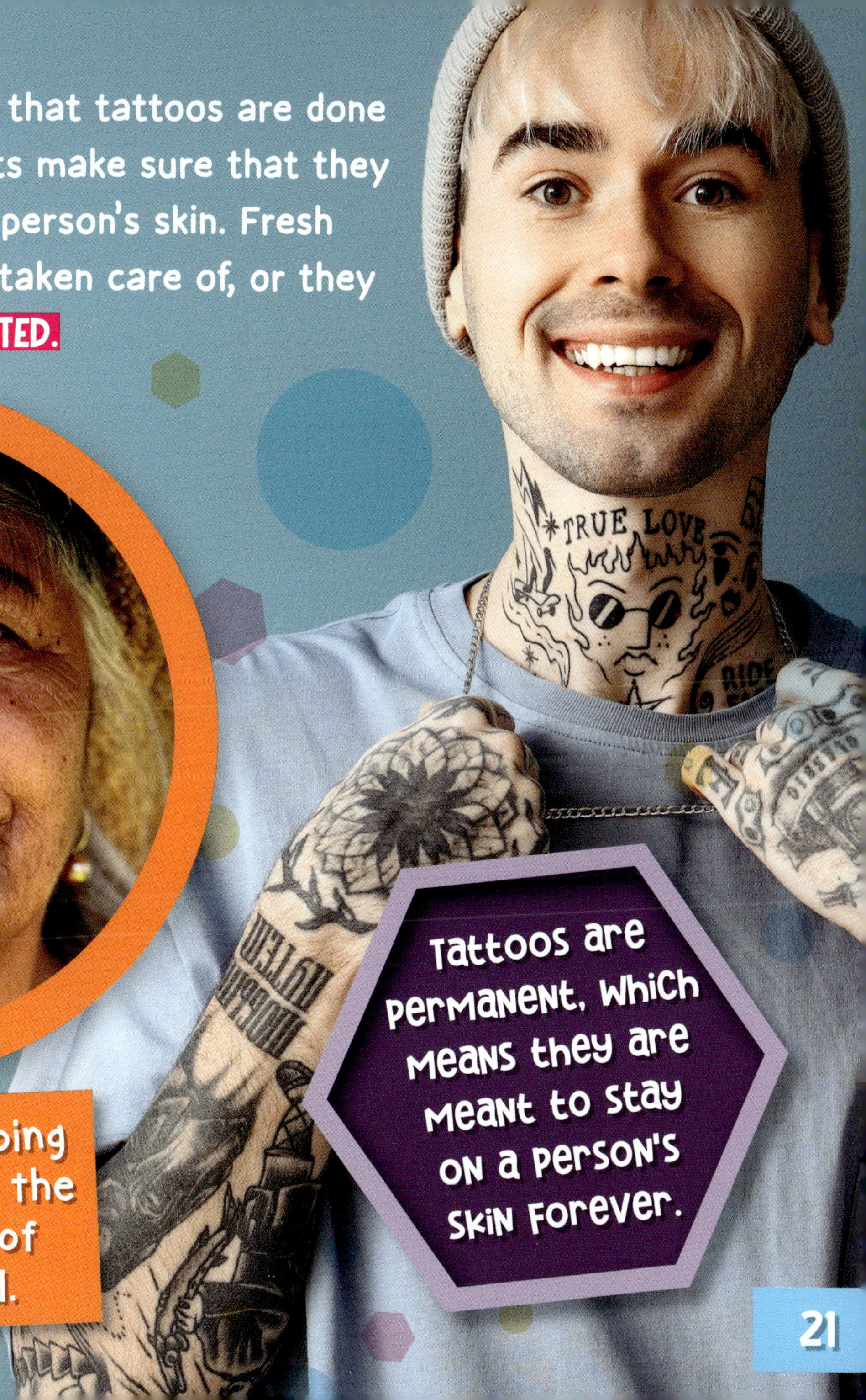

Tattoos are permanent, which means they are meant to stay on a person's skin forever.

WHAT ABOUT YOUR SKIN?

Skin is amazing! There are so many different colors and textures. All skin is beautiful, and it is part of what makes us unique.

Always wear sunscreen to protect your skin from the sun.

What is your skin like? Is it tan or fair? Do you have any freckles or moles? Remember, your skin is special, and so are you!

GLOSSARY

allergic reactions
when the body thinks a harmless substance, such as nuts, is harmful and creates feelings of sickness because of it

condition
a health issue or illness

contagious
able to spread from one person to another

culture
the traditions, ideas, and ways of life of a group of people

heals
becomes healthy or whole again

infected
when germs or disease have entered part of the body

natural
found in nature and not made by people

personality
the ways a person acts that make them different to other people

shades
darker or lighter versions of a color

texture
the feel and look of something

unique
unlike anything or anyone else

INDEX